SIXTEEN PAINTERS OF

THE YOUNG SCHOOL
OF PARIS

Edited by J. C. Lambert
Photographs by Luc Joubert
Translated by Haakon Chevalier

HUBERT JUIN

SIXTEEN PAINTERS OF
THE YOUNG SCHOOL
OF PARIS

Sixteen reproductions

THE POCKET MUSEUM

GOLDEN GRIFFIN BOOKS, ARTS, INC.

WHEN Paul Klee, at the age of thirty-five, embarked for Kairwan, he did not yet know that he was a painter, any more than he suspected what the future held in store for him. What the future held in store for him, as it happened, was nothing less than this: that he would open new horizons for painting. There is in Klee a perpetual gentleness. He always gives free rein to his heart. He is quite naturally a moralist and quite naturally popular. And if he sometimes forgets to be intelligent, it is for our greater joy: he never forgets to be just. And with a justness that solicits us, composed of fidelity, seriousness, generosity. Yes, these are virtues for which painters, and not writers only, must be asked to give accounting. In this realm all will be saved by generosity, by give and take, or will be forever lost.

In Paul Klee's writings are to be found a few phrases of the highest tenor. One day he jots down: *to be abstract with memories*. He does not trust the mirages of geometry, and recomposes the lessons of history for his own purposes. The discovery of the triangle, of the square, of the circle, that whole realm of form that has been developed and that is assuredly

7

intoxicating does not, Paul Klee is quite aware, prevent one from being human. And in his great laconicism (this can be judged by the signs that the painter uses), he will be careful at all times and above all, while he is painting, to forget all method. *There is no substitute for intuition*, he says, and nothing is more true when, at every moment, painting is to be brought into being and made to bear witness, at every moment, to the savor of the world. *One learns to know something by the root, one learns the prehistory of the visible. But this is not yet art on the highest level. On the highest level the mysterious begins.*

This we recognize today: the reasons of the eye are the reason of men as well. Painting is not an idle game. It is a way of being in the world. Which means that is has a place among the major arts that are the arts of affirmation. It is a risk, to be sure, but it is also a commitment. It is a surface offered to the light, as who could deny? But it is also depth, and depth in which man is recomposed.

It is language. Contemporary experiments have shown the flexibility and the riches of this language. A spot is no longer a spot, is not even, when the painter makes it emerge from the white canvas, a sign, but an affirmation of the spirit, of the hand that creates, of the man before his task. Klee himself —to confine ourselves to him—once he is sure of his vocation (I and color have become one, I am a painter !) will not stop until he is able to transpose the rhythms of his creative undertaking into his pictorial space. He will modulate the colors to such a point that by this very means he will create distance. It will be observed that blue comes forward, that gray withdraws, that sight trembles in the light of the sun. Klee is like

Cézanne: they both know that *nature is within*, a laconic expression that signifies that the miracle of art springs from an eternal confrontation and a unique whole. Between the painter and his model the work of art is born. And nowhere else.

When Klee set out for Kairwan he was already in possession of his genius. And this genius, make no mistake, is linked to popular expressions. The unique place that has been accorded this painter is due to the fact that he does not set himself up against reality, but on the contrary participates with all his fibres in the savor of the real world. He is an enchanter, and quite the contrary of a rebel. He is a painter, and a great one, which means the opposite of an entertainer. It is well to think of him when one speaks of painting: Paul Klee stands for health, and the love of life, and the thirst for happiness. Not for a moment does he dream of compromising *the great octave of creation*. In truth, he is enchanted to participate in this great octave, knowing that no voice is lost. Our young painters sometimes omit pleasure. They are wrong: in the history of painting, they are the first to be able to give themselves to it wholly. As they are the first to be able, likewise, to incarnate the satiric dimensions of the art of painting. They are the contemporaries of the bursting of fixed forms. This is not negligible. They are likewise the contemporaries of a most strange conspiracy: the conspiracy of the arts...

For several centuries peinters and literary men lived, in relation each to the other, in the strictest isolation. The arts were narrowly compartmentalized. Verbal undertakings had nothing in common with visual undertakings. Between them there was no possibility of synthesis. This appeared all the more clearly in the case of a few exceptional personalities who attempted to express themselves on both levels, and who did in fact express themselves *on both levels*, but without anything passing from one to the other, as though not one but two distinct individuals were concerned. To be sure, when we look back on those remote periods we find no difficulty in making the synthesis ; in discovering, for example, that the Breughel of the *Fall of Icarus* is nothing other than a kind of Montaigne.

In so doing, it is we who are surprising, not history. It is we who are surprising with respect to Breughel and with respect to Montaigne, and not the first in the eyes of the second. It is true that we are excusable and that there occurred, about a century ago, a fairly unusual phenomenon. A century ago an attempt was made to discover the laws, the process, that would make possible (it was thought) in the immediate the synthesis that we make *a posteriori*.

Writers and painters did in fact imagine themselves to have a common destiny. Baudelaire studied pictorial works with an attention unknown up to that time. In *Aesthetic Curiosities* we see less the operation of an avidity of the mind than the impulse of a passion in every respect similar to that which the author of the *Flowers of Evil* put into poetry. Zola studied his former fellow-student of Aix, and undertook to write *The Work of Art*. He had not understood the first thing about Cézanne? I grant you this, but it is of no importance. Baudelaire, too, preferred to be silent when confronted with Manet. Now the sign of the synthesis I am speaking of, the about-turn, the reversal of painting, the fulfillment of Goya's will, however strange, is unmistakable: it is *Olympia*.

10

How hard it is for us to understand today the scandal unleashed by that amiable burgher who was a frequenter of Tortoni's terrace! And see, at the same time, another scandal in the making, which in this case affected Literature: Mallarmé, an obscure poet living on the Rue de Rome, observed in writing *Igitur*, that in probing verse to its depth the poet discovers his own death. By a singular conjunction, the best work of Manet is undoubtedly that *Portrait of Mallarmé*, which by itself alone founds the glories of poetry in painting.

Is what we have here a drama of expression? If you will. Let us steer clear of the concept of tragedy: crisis of expression is more accurate. At this moment it seems that everything has been written, everything said, everything attempted. Likewise, nothing has escaped the painter's eye. The whole world, the landscapes, the passions—everything that is to be found within a class conception has been described, set down, immortalized. A young man feels the writer's calling. What is he to do? Behind him, the *Human Comedy* blocks the horizon. About him, pressing him from all sides: Zola's *Rougon* series and the Goncourt brothers' novels. If this young man bears the name of Jules Renard, he will challenge literature and, within this class convention, will make it burst and practically disappear. If his name is Marcel Proust, he will write *Swann's Way*, that Olympia of Letters. Even so, it was necessary for Proust to meet Bergson...

You can see what I am getting at: this crisis of expression made it necessary for art to rebel against class convention and escape from it. This revolution held out a virgin world. Everything had to be named, everything had to be painted as though nothing had ever been painted or named. One frequented the museums only in order to observe *treatments*. Aside from which one could only contemplate deserted works. The savor of the universe had again passed over to the side of life and was again offered for the conquest of the arts. And an alluring theroy on this theme could be imagined: the savor of life absorbed by art, then, as a result of a revolution, restored to life to be again absorbed by art. Such is not the case, however, and this for the reason that culture tends to universalize itself at the same time that, having become better known, the past ceases to be the expression (a menacing one) of a series of imperative ideas to become a quasi infinite succession of assumed risks, of individual expressions, of *incarnations*. The more universal culture becomes, the more the ancient schools lose their rigor and their meaning: the sclerosis that they are said to represent gives way to the mobility of individuals. It is difficult indeed to imagine, today, a *Quarrel of the Ancients and the Moderns*. And what has the Museum become for modern man if not a witness—and a witness that can, on occasion (and there is no lack of occasions), become brotherly. No longer the rule, and the syntax, as it were, of a class convention.

There used to be schools. We are beginning to perceive that henceforth there are only painters. In our young school of Paris, it seems that there are no painters of spots (for example), but—each time—a confrontation between the painter and the work through the intermediary of this exploded matter.

But what about the abstract? it will be asked. And, more precisely, what about the experiments of these young painters?

12

That is what we were getting at. For a long time, I confess, I believed that abstract art was the ideal refuge of the famous class conception. Rather than see the world as it is, the bourgeoisie much preferred not to see the world at all. I still believe this is more or less the case of the society "abstractionists", more strictly and totally domesticated than the vilest of the figurative painters. But to confine oneself to such an overall judgment would be infantile and could satisfy only the limited intelligence of a few littérateurs more Marxist than life. In reality, the abstract painting that we see came into being with de Staël rather than with Kandinsky, with Soulages rather than with Mondrian, with Carrey rather than with Magnelli, in other words the painting that, wishing to subdue form, directly and resolutely tackles the myths of the world and takes in a whole moral fullness, this painting, ever in search of its true vocabulary, does not have its place beyond the universe. It calls upon the great voices of the plant world and of the earth, the night, the day, the sacred, that which devours man and that which pacifies him. It is no longer simply language, it is likewise the will to language. It is seen to match itself against expression and against the impossibility of communication. It is known to be generous. It may be thought unforgetable. *It is.*

And this has absolutely nothing to do with a functional art. The object is to be abstract with memories. But what memories? They form a procession going back to prehistory. They have their origins in the caves. They tell us of the conquest of fire. And a word recurs throughout this mythology: man, man, man—to such a point that what we have is no longer mythology but Truth.

13

The health of a painter can be judged by the pleasure of the matter and by the anguish of the hand: these two concrete data cannot be effaced from a picture. It is they that we first read. Inevitably. And this art differs profoundly from the impetus given by Kandinsky, by Malevitch, by Mondrian: *it is not a search for an aesthetic*. It would rather confess to being a search for a morality. It is interested not so much by beauty as by discourse. And what is discourse if not communication first of all? The place of this painting is not so much the Museum as the City. It is concerned with the relations that men have established among themselves. Now these relations are bankrupt. A new morality, pure of myths, must be born. A morality of true men. Herein lies the greatness of these investigations.

I do not wish, however, to introduce a tragic note, especially into something that is dominated by pleasure. We know that the pleasure of painting and the pleasure of writing are recent conquests. Man, the artist, no longer has to hide beneath the unnameable clouds of the romantics, beneath the unnamed passions of the symbolists. He can be proud of his work without having to apologize for it.

It may perhaps seem that I am trying to provide the young painters of today with masters. I am not. They have only one master—an obscure one—and that is history. I simply would like to observe, in connection with this young school of Paris and the examples that it proposes to us, that abstract art has ceased to be an aesthetic. This is what saves it both from being a diversion and from dispersal. One thing at least appears to me to be common to these young painters: an ascetic spirit, one might say. A way of affirming themselves in history and in time—without flinching before the consequences.

Let us come back to the scandal of Manet. *Olympia* has nothing about it to surprise *us*. Any more than does the *Luncheon on the grass*. And we should readily admit to being rather embarrassed by Manet's way of painting after ancient models, by his manner—quite his own—of frankly beginning again what has already been done in times past. But what we must not fail to note is this: in his eyes, though in an obscure way, nothing has yet been done. Painting has yet to be born. And if this is valid and true for every painter, if every painter is, each time he paints, the birth of painting, this is only since *Olympia*, in other words quite exactly since the collapse and the rejection of orthodoxy. Henceforth only the heretical painter, in giving birth to painting, saves painting. And the scandal of *Olympia* is precisely that: heresy avowed, accomplished, unveiled. In the realm of the arts orthodoxy bears a name: it is the sum of the rules that are the foundation of an aesthetic in relation to a given conception of the world. It is an aesthetic canon... *Olympia* falls outside the aesthetic canon that centuries had contributed to forge. Let us say that this was the bourgeois canon, the bourgeois aesthetic, the ideal illustration of a bourgeois conception of the world.

One of the principal characteristics of the bourgeois world is idealism. The mission of painting is to idealize. And above all, to idealize the model. The superior genre here is the portrait. It is proper that Mr. Prud'homme should be immortalized, in a toga and holding the sword of justice in his hand.

15

As for Mr. Prud'homme's mistress (Miss I'm For Sale), she will become Venus. It must be noted that naïveté is on *Olympia's* side. Manet casts upon Victorine, and at the same time on the canvases of the Museum, a virgin gaze. Couture, on the other hand, does not. And the public of the time that contemplated Giorgione with rapt admiration uttered loud cries before the modern costumes of Manet's people. In Olympia there is a black cat. It seems to have stepped directly out of a poem by Baudelaire. It plays an important role, for Manet would undoubtedly have been forgiven a great deal if he had replaced it by some lion or leopard. There is a bourgeois *Bestiary*. Manet failed to respect it. The cat, as is well known, is too close to slippers for anyone who has no sense of poetry. Moreover, Victorine is not, for example, Tintoretto's *Suzanne*. Yet the chaste Suzanne, on whose sex eyes are riveted, Suzanne, whose nudity is twice outraged because already profaned within the painting itself by the old men, Suzanne shocks none of the noble sentiments that are in Mr. Prud'homme's soul. That poor Victorine, on the other hand, that no-account boy who posed for the *Fife-player?* People could not find enough insults to fling at *Olympia!* Is this not rather odd?

Tintoretto's *Suzanne* is both ideal beauty and ideal eroticism. That flesh reflected in the water is, to tell the truth, too firm, too harmonious. Love, and especially venal love (the great tabu of the bourgeoisie that none the less marries off its daughters for "advantages"), rape, to be quite blunt, cannot disturb the lines of this perfection. This Suzanne is chaste because, were she impure, she would no longer be Suzanne. She is ideal, better yet: idealized. Olympia, on the other hand, is offered. She appeals to all those obscurities that Suzanne

16

refuses, that Suzanne denies. Yet let us look closely: it is Suzanne who is impure, because the old men whom Tintoretto has painted possess her more surely (and we too, through them, possess her more erotically) than it is possible to possess Olympia. For Olympia is pleasure. And the work of Manet, the pleasure of painting.

Proust would remember this, to good purpose, when he came to describe Elstir, that painter of blended sea and landscapes.

And if over so many centuries painters and writers separately pursued their investigations, in the strictest isolation, it is quite apparent that such is no longer the case in our day. They do not need to join forces in order to respond to the same exigencies. They quite naturally share the same destiny. And this above all: the conquest of reality.

Man is no longer in the position of trembling before the universe. He knows how to tame, to his advantage, the voices and the forces that even yesterday terrorized him. If he has understood that progress is neither a new divinity nor an indefinite and continuous line, he also knows that it is by successive leaps, by risks ceaselessly assumed and renewed, that he can achieve a greater mastery of himself and of the external world. These risks—painting, writing—he daily accepts. And each day, through him, for him, the world comes into being. It is no longer so much to painting that the artist must, at every moment, give birth, but to the entire universe. *And through pleasure.*

We must, I believe, be suspicious of philosophical criticism. What could such criticism say about this handful of painters united by the same realism of intention and by the same expressionism of intention? The philosopher would be wrong and the painter right. To him who *does*, and to none other, belongs the transformation of the world. Such a one among them will have no truck with space; will claim that the obvious elements in the realm of form are the vertical line and the horizontal line; will add that all he wants to do is paint without detracting anything from the real. And what if we see something else?... Another will aim, by meams of the pictorial vocabulary, to create a myth. He will blend the avowal of a dream with the requirements of reality. Still another will undertake some wild investigation. All will find refuge and peace in the poetic faculty. This is a great sign.

A sign first of all of this: painting has ceased to be the art of adorning the walls of our boudoirs or our hovels. Painting is today a way of breathing, of keeping oneself intact, of refusing to disappear, and—quite frankly—of being a nuisance.

Young painters often affect not to go to the Museum. To begin with: they do go. The statements they make to newspapermen are false on this point. They have gone and looked. They have seen—and seen well. They will all say (perhaps) that they have nothing to do with Manet. Nonsense!... They have to do—and intimately—with Manet, with Goya, with Piero della Francesca, with Masaccio, with Cézanne. And more, assuredly, than with Kandinsky or Mondrian.

Manet was not an isolated case. It happens that it was upon *Olympia* that the historic role we know devolved. Soon the mountain of Sainte-Victoire and the vicinity of the Black

Castle were to enable Cézanne, in turn, to bring about a modification in painting. And what a strange man this was! He is generally credited with a naïveté that he did not possess, while the naïveté that is properly his is no less generally unrecognized. Cézanne was by no means unsophisticated. He knew the Museum as well as Manet. But he had the same naïveté as he: that which is established between the painter and the virginity, and the ingenuousness, of the white canvas. He opened a door to painting, opened it once and for all. After him, every true painter was to find himself obliged to create his own space. The sign of painting was to become that very thing: space. And the enigmatic role of the mirror that we see in *Suzanne at the bath* will now be better unsderstood. It will be seen that it is this mirror that contributes chiefly to the erotization of the painting, and that it is by the space thus (and treacherously) opened that the rape made possible by the two old men is accomplished. The sign of painting has indeed changed! For Manet as for Cézanne, rape was of little consequence. It was no longer an issue.

It was to become an issue again, later, in the architectures of surrealism, when painting, from having tried to lean too heavily on literature, collapsed, teetered, lost the best of itself: that savor, precisely, which is the savor of the universe. And which, strictly speaking, is poetry.

Cézanne did not know Bergson. There is a sentence, however, in *The Immediate Data of Consciousness*, that enables us to come closer to the secret of the painter from Aix: "Each of the successive states of the external world exists in itself, and their multiplicity has reality only for a consciousness, capable of storing them first of all, then of juxtaposing them, exteriorizing the ones in relation to the others." Cézanne's long, patient investigation seems to have been concerned with the analysis of space according to the angle of duration. His success is bound up with the fact that he achieved, by the very process of analysis, a synthesis of vision.

Much has been said about Cézanne and his influence, about pictorial space and its mysteries. Too much, it appears. It is often said nowadays that whoever speaks of painting is indulging in literature—and by literature is meant *a great stir over nothing!* And yet it is possible to see in the contemporary pictorial adventure an extreme attempt to shatter the traditional limits of painting, that is to say to cease to consider painting as exclusively an art of representation. Kandinsky was to find his ideal in music, Mondrian in architecture. There is something touching in the purpose of these precursors!

And already a new crisis of expression is becoming defined. It has to do with the obligation in which the painter finds himself each time to give birth to painting. It has to do also with the prime imperative that, since Cézanne, dominates artistic destinies; each painter sees himself called upon to create his own space. These two necessities introduce the painter to the center, to the very heart of the confusion of the arts. He will participate in literature, in architecture, in music. He will be inclined to seek the conditions of a functional art, participating in the savor of life without thereby absorbing this savor. He will refuse to seek true Life in art or outside of art. There is no longer for him any outside. The work is integrated in society itself and finds its place and function in the day-today life of the community. The morrows of the Soviet Revolution came very close, during the reign of the N.E.P. and under the aegis of Lunacharsky, to making of this dream a reality. But no such thing happened.

No such thing happened, for the very reason that art is not a function but a discourse. Painting does not serve, but says. At best, in the Community, it is a great liberating voice. But it does not thereby cease to be an accusing voice. Cassandra today would be a painter. In this connection we need only think of the chair with the straw seat and the shoes painted by Van Gogh, which like a piercing cry rend not only the weft of a certain historic condition but also accuse, reject, compromise the very order of Creation. On the walls of Charleville Rimbaud wrote: *"Merde à Dieu."* It is true that we are at a moment when the crisis of expression is linked to a general crisis of civilization. Culture is challenged by contributions (cultural ones, as it happens) from worlds formerly unknown or despised. There are no more savages. It has taken ethnographers some time to realize it, and Lévy-Bruhl has timidly confided to his *Notebooks* that he was mistaken and that there exists no pre-logical mentality. From Frobenius to Lévi-Strauss, to Michel Leiris, to Otto Klineberg, the universe unveils itself, offers itself, rediscovers its lost unity. It is necessary to speak for all. The torments of the writer and the torments of the painter converge (they are the same), and in solitude seek to discover a true language.

Figurative? Abstract? What a stupid quarrel. Dozens of so-called "abstract" painters may be mentioned who have been able to keep themselves pure of all formalism. Dozens of "figurative" painters can be mentioned who have succumbed to the most odious formalism. The only ones who count are the man who is behind the canvas (so to speak) and the man who contemplates it. Our age, at least, will have the merit of having purged men's spirit of Prometheism and of vague and ill-assured sentiments. We know ourselves better. And we are also able to measure at its true value what is human in a work. We leave the gods in peace, for creation, whatever has been said, is not the work of gods but the work of men. And knowing this has enabled us to work out the rules of an ethic of daily life. The artist is no longer prey to the delirium of the pythoness. The artist has a man's duties. A few fretful spirits hanker after past illusions. They do not perceive that one must ceaselessly choose between myth and truth. This choice, precisely this choice, is being accomplished by the present young painters.

When one or another declares (and I imagine that among those who are commented upon below there will be at least one) that he intends only to paint and to do nothing else, we feel that he is like *le Bourgeois gentilhomme*, and that he sins by a refusal to define the very thing he is doing.

I regret that I am unable to express myself as an art critic would. But it seems to me that today art is much more important than art itself. It has changed signs. It has broken with uselessness while rediscovering the pleasure of the act. Before his white canvas our young painter is joyous. No monster dominates him. He is alone. He is free. This supreme good is, at the same time, pitiless. The painter who falls short is quickly judged. The operation of this judgment takes place within himself. It is no longer society that takes measures against him, it is his own conscience. And if he has nothing to say, he will have no choice but to be silent, however much he may wish to continue to shine.

And what if all of them, without exception, were mistaken? What if this present venture was doomed? What if they were all headed down a blind alley? However difficult it is to imagine such a situation, certain critics asusme it, maintain that the young generation has definitely lost its way, that nothing can now save it. So be it ! And even the greatest error does not prevent, does not obliterate the thrill of what has been expressed, were it but one single time ; of what has risen to the throb of speech, were it but for a second ; of what has encountered the great pleasure of utterance. Error does not abolish. It stresses. I remember a remark of Mounier's: *A life is not broken that has borne great witness*. These words should be present to the minds of all who undertake a generous venture.

People honorably known for their level-headedness shrug their shoulders before the examples of this young painting and say, "A lot of foolishness !" And these little words that they utter with gravity, with assurance, invariably make me think of another sentence, which occurs in *The Brothers Karamazov*, where Dostoyevski shows Aliosha and his brother Dmitri conversing. "I have committed a blunder, according to your ideas, a foolishness according to the world, but it could be that this foolishness is at the present time the only salvation for all of us !" This is a second sentence that I advise creators to remember. It is better, in art, to commit *a foolishness according to the world* than to founder in formalism and sclerosis.

Van Gogh led a dramatic existence. He was a boon to literature. He gave birth to a myth. Cézanne, on the other
hand, was everyday. What dreariness in that existence,
undermined, rent day in and day out by the pettiness of a small
provincial town! But also, there is nothing here that is not
above all resolution of painting. He disappears in the gigantic
succession of works. He did more than see the world anew.
He invented man at the same time. An admirer of Poussin,
he could have claimed to stem from Vauvenargues. He was
the first to modify landscape as he pleased, abolishing the three
or four kilometers that separate Sainte-Victoire from the
Aqueduct. In this respect he went farther than Courbet. But
the difference does not lie simply in the lack of respect for the
external world. Courbet acting as we know with faggots
(Look, those black spots on my painting are faggots!), and
Cézanne rearranging the surroundings of Aix, are in no way
similar. What Courbet might have divined Cézanne accom-
plishes. He does not hesitate to place his work on two planes
simultaneously. On the one hand, reality comes and pierces
his canvas like a hurled stone. On the other, his operation on
reality endows his work with architecture. A canvas by
Cézanne is at the same time what is and what Cézanne wants
that there be. Between the objective reality and the painter's
discourse appears the new space of the pictorial universe. It
has often been said that the too-long arm of the *Boy With Red
Vest* was an error in perpective. Cézanne's contemporaries,
who made the observation, saw badly: that too-long arm is
already modern painting. There was no longer any question
of scandal. People said of Cézanne that he did "dirty painting", but they laughed at *Olympia*. There is a continuous line,
however, that connects Manet's negro woman with *Scipio*.

24

It had to be perceived.   At the moment when it was perceived, the existence of another art—negro art, specifically—was also perceived.

But what Cézanne seemed to discover at this moment was that there is no object, that there is only time.   Certain young painters who were later to be discovered would not, I imagine, take issue with such an observation.

Guillaume Apollinaire who, like Rimbaud, was so fond of overdoors* that the discovery of Rousseau the customs officer was for him more than a revelation, succeeded in quelling in himself the voices of literature to a sufficient degree to be able to turn with a certain abnegation to painters.   His first enthusiasm: *fauvism*.   At last—he would say—we are now masters of nature and perhaps we shall never cease to invent new colors.   They soon ceased to invent new colors, and there was no more talk of anarchy but, with the rigors of the great period of cubism, of order.   Braque discovered, at the same time as the splendid scaffoldings of the *Bach Aria*, the climate of the pre-Socratics.   Heraclitus, called the Obscure, when he noted "the sun is the zise of a man's foot", surely did not suspect that he was later to contribute to demythizing and to demystifying painting.   But when in 1907, in his harlequins' studio of the Bateau Lavoir, Picasso—a small Spaniard who drank his *café-crème* in a bistrot at that time unknown, the *Rotonde*—showed the Young Ladies of Avignon to his friends, a page of history had just been concluded and another chapter

---

* The decoration sometimes found above door frames.

begun.   In this chapter we are.   And with us, more or less attentive, more or less lucid spectators, are likewise all these young painters determined to speak truly and who are today about thirty, that is to say who find themselves, in the bitter words of the poet, midway on the road of life.

It is given to no one to be the historian of his own time. Each one, here, is a dramatis persona, and nothing more.   But nothing less.

Everything that is in the bud in the most flagrant contradictions of our time is not necessarily compromised by these very contradictions.   I seem to perceive in the experiments of our young painters a desire to go beyond individual expression. This individual expression is linked, for that matter, to the worst of mythologies.   To be sure, it is not a question of diluting the individual (artist) in a crowd (of artists).   It is a question of ensuring to communication, to the powers of the work over reality, the greatest possible sharpness.   The conquest of reality by the adventures of the eye will become one of the richest and the most absorbing chapters of contemporary history.

It might undoubtedly be said here that the young painters are in the first phase of the battle that they must wage.   They have perhaps not yet reached the point of dominating the real. Who can claim this?   But if they are beginning already to dominate reality, it is in a manner that is still obscure and incompletely dissociated from that *prehistory of the visible* of which Paul Klee spoke.   What they are in the process of effecting is a revolution—in the strict sense of the word.   Karl Marx

26

analyzed in a remarkable way a fundamental datum of the human condition. Many Marxist theses had to be verified by history, and the undesrtanding of Marx (through the influence of first-rate minds, such as Georg Lukacs or Henri Lefebvre) had to become clearer, less abstract, less theoretical, before it became at last possible to conceive that the concept of alienation is unquestionably the key concept in this interpretation of the world and of history. I purposely quote Lukacs and Lefebvre, for Marx has been chiefly considered by economists. The two Marxist philosophers, on the other hand, if they are in no way contemptuous of the economic views of Marxism (quite the contrary), have nevertheless wished to apply the consequences of the dialectic to the various aspects of men's activity.

It happens that the concept of alienation—brought out by them, and by a non-Marxist philosopher, Mounier—is a complex concept. To an economic alienation corresponds a spiritual alienation, and vice versa. It may be concluded, at the extreme, that the Revolution must be at the same time economic and spiritual, or be ineffective. Must promote at the same time a new distribution of production goods and of consumer goods and a new morality. Must ensure the possibility of living, but also dignity.

The class convention that, up to the scandal of *Olympia*, prevailed in the realm of representation, was the sign of a spiritual alienation (to which, moreover, corresponded an economic alienation, visible among the painters of the nineteenth century who were not favored by fortune at birth). It was not enough for *Olympia* to cause a scandal to put an end

27

to the alienation. This alienation survived, and still survives, in formalism. It has become incarnated—royally, it must be said—in abstract art. It was again attacked, but to the detriment of painting itself, by the surrealists. The painters close to our hearts have their hearts set on vanquishing alienation once and for all. And if every great artistic success is a victory over alienation, it should be observed that our time— which is is eminently a time of contradiction—lends itself less than any other to the *fairness* of the struggle against alienation. Where, exactly, is alienation in this realm? On what rules, precisely, is one to base oneself? Which side is one to choose?

Only generosity can here serve as a guide. He who is generous does not desire only his own liberty. He alone speaks for all, can claim to speak for all. And it is the painter who aims at the maximum of communication, at the maximum of freedom, at the greatest amplitude of discourse, it is he who aims at the most powerful work, it is he who gives proof of the greatest generosity, it is he who, most effectively, combats the spiritual alienation that is in language. In the language of the writer as well as in this language that is composed of forms and colors.

September 1956.

The non-figurative painters have refused once and for all to reproduce reality as the social eye, that of the camera, records it. Hunters of new images, they have set out on an adventure that will lead them, and us with them, whither? Beyond the petty occasional aesthetics, this book seeks to present an open and unprejudiced account of their explorations in 1956, a first meeting. The adventure continues. Until next year!

J. C. L.

PIERRE ALECHINSKY

1927 : born in Brussels.   1944 : studies in Ensaad.   1947 : Galerie Lou Cosyn, Brussels, Jeune Peinture Belge group.   1948 : « Les Mains Eblouies », Galerie Maeght, and Galerie Apollo, Brussels.   1949 : Cobra movement.   1950 : « Les Mains Eblouies », Prix Hélène Jacquet, Prix Jeune Peinture Belge.   1951 : settles in Paris.   1952 : Atelier 17. 1953 : Galerie Martinet, Amsterdam.   1954 : Galerie Nina Dausset. 1955 : Palais des Beaux-Arts, Brussels.

What is happening?   It is as if life had taken refuge in painting (at the same time convulsing it), I see more of it in Alechinsky's paintings than in the newspapers...   Is this spirit of contradiction a law of painting?   Even yesterday, many traces of it were to be found ; today it can be said to be a kind of relay: painting takes over what we have abandoned in everyday life: the avowal, the contact, the charter, the respect for the indivisible.

It is too bad that criticism often takes sides with our time against this painting.   It brings painting to its knees and, instead of liking it, or detesting it, that is to say participating in it, enslaves it ; the more naked painting is, the more criticism goes out of its way to dress it up, the more it lends it ; and on such knees paintings make one think of those the more it lends it ; and on such knees painting make one think of those straw puppets by means of which ventriloquists hold dialogues with themselves.

Everyone writes as though the painter were guilty, and he must by all means be justified ; does he really have to be guilty to be strong?   Far from it !   The painter's hands are not dirty, nor are the poet's.   Even though language gets bogged down in the Assemblies, and colors in the Schools, the poet speaks truly, and so does the painter: I am thinking of Alechinsky.   He has something that is rather rare: he does not believe that painting comes closer to life by becoming more distant from painting.   A little painting draws us away from reality, Colombus said, while much painting brings us close to it.   And Alechinsky does not attempt to escape problems by vomiting them up, he assumes them ; he knows that if painting is not a penitence, neither is it a farce.

CHRISTIAN DOTREMONT.

WINTER - 60″ × 40″ - 1951.

FRANÇOIS ARNAL

Born October 2, 1924 in La Valette (Var). Spent his whole child-hood in the country Went to school at the Toulon lycée; studied law and literature at the University of Aix en Provence. Began to paint in 1940, and settled in Paris in 1948. Principal one-man exhibits: 1950: Galerie Drouant-David; 1951, Galerie Parnass, Wuppertal (Germany); 1953, Galerie Craven and British Council, Glasgow (Scotland); 1954, Galleria del Naviglio, Milan; 1955, Galerie Parnass, Wuppertal; Neuenkirchen (Saar), Palais des Beaux-Arts, Brussels, and Galerie Rive droite; 1956, Galerie Cavallino, Venice. Numerous group expositions, including « Les Murs Vivants » (1949), « Les Mains Eblouies » (1949 and 1950), Biennial of Menton (1951), Salon de Mai (1952), « Un Art Autre » (1952), « Phases de l'Art Contemporain » (1955-56), etc.

Arnal as a child had what is conventionally called a gift. He painted the event of the *Wine Harvest* as he himself felt it. His painting was spontaneous, hieroglyphic, as the drawing of children is, but with the original and native temperament of the born painter. Having come to manhood, Arnal was quite aware that there were other techniques, and that one could not indefinitely content oneself with the paradise green of childhood. He experienced bitter moments when one doubts oneself, when painting, rather than joy, becomes pain. This "descent into hell", as Tapié says, preceded a magnificent reascension to the light, and to this reascension, to this unveiling of a luminous sense, too immediately bright not to be dark as mystery in broad daylight, the recent great canvases bear witness.

JEAN HYPPOLITE.

32

CROSSING THE BEREZINA - *80″ × 80″ - 1955.*

GIANNI BERTINI

Born in Pisa (Italy) in 1922. He has a Doctor's degree in mathematics. A figurative painter, he was one of the first in Italy to turn, in 1947, to abstraction. He settled in Paris in 1951. One-man shows: 1948, Salto Gallery, Milan; 1950, Naviglio Gallery, Milan; 1951, San Fedele Gallery, Milan, Cavallino Gallery, Venice, Numero Gallery, Florence. 1953 and 54, Palace of Fine Arts, Brussels, 1954. Galerie Arnaud, Paris, 1956; Dome Gallery, Copenhagen and Long Wharf Studio, Boston, May Salon, 1954. Venice Biennial, 1951. Numerous group exhibits. Published in 1951, in Venice, a theoretical work, « Prologuo per un Arte attuale ».

Against a background that is often purple—the very color of legend—an exuberant panoramic weft is woven in glassy yarns that unites the different biological and historic *reigns*. One thinks of a show in which a single non-Euclidian continuum would juxtapose, without a break, the moment when the Iron Crown sinks into the rock and the one when the Titanic sinks into the deep. An Invincible Armada of steel and quartz cruises within sight of coral reefs —reefs unforeseeably tossed up by the palette knife, in blackish spines in the heart of ethereal structures. Bertini permits himself thus, from time to time, to draw the attention of the beholder back to the purely plastic side of the work. But the poetic element remains predominant in his approach, which couples, in short-circuits generating durable storms, the most disparate realities in time and structure. In him we witness the analogical symbiosis of barbaric splendors of long ago, of hypothetical fauna and of themes tuned to the most vertiginous immediate: atomic disintegration, supersonic speed, etc. Thus, by his search for a fertile collision between several principles or substances that are very different, his undertaking is related to the permanent temptations of surrealism. But on the other hand it wholly escapes the vogue for the pure informal, whose inanity at present arouses a certain zeal. Neither didactic nor decorative, Bertini's painting strives passionately toward poetic and dynamising intervention in the too often stagnant world of non-figuration and of automatism.

EDOUARD JAGUER.

THE HORRORS OF CRISSA - *36″ × 29″ - 1957 - Collection L. I.*

MARTIN BARRÉ

Born in 1925 in Nantes. School of Fine Arts of Nantes, from 1939 to 1943. Non-figurative painting since 1950. One-man shows: Galerie Michel Columb, Nantes, 1946; Galerie du Vert-Galant, Paris, 1949; Galerie La Roue, Paris, 1955 and 1956. Salons: Réalités nouvelles, 1955 and 1956; Automne, Lyon, 1955. Numerous group exhibits, including « Eloge du Petit Format » and « Présent du Bleu » at the Galerie la Roue.

Since his first exposition of abstract painting (Paris, 1954), Martin Barré has steadily continued to affirm his style. He today enjoys a very special situation among the painters of his generation.

While he first limited his colors to white, red ochre and blue (which nevertheless allowed him to obtain a very wide gamut, passing through the grays and browns), he has now introduced other colors in his compositions, and his whites range from the dazzling to the unctuous.

Martin Barré, who works slowly, prudently, meticulously, clings to this restriction on his palette. He is of those who believe, with André Gide, that "art is born of constraints and dies of liberties".

Even as the rectilinear landscapes of Holland have been compared to Mondrian's geometric paintings, it has been said that there was a strange similarity between certain paintings of Barré and aerial views of harbors and ports. This is because the most abstract forms always "remember" obsessional images. Mondrian remained as Dutch as Vermeer, and Martin Barré of Nantes transmutes the memories of the port of his childhood and his love of things of the sea.

MICHEL RAGON.

36

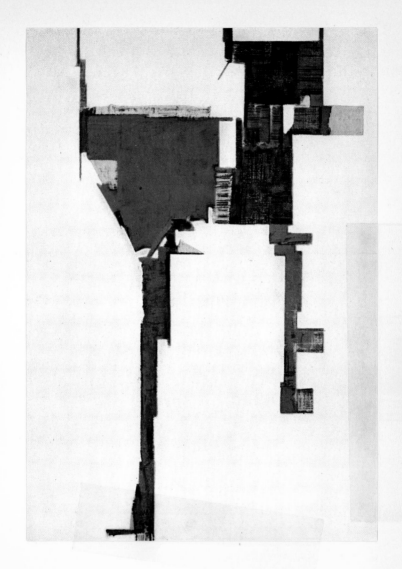

COMPOSITION - *32" × 24" - 1956.*

HUGUETTE - ARTHUR BERTRAND

*Born near Paris. Her family originated in the South of France
and in Auvergne. Conventional schooling. First paintings in 1942.
Worked in the Grande Chaumière studio, then in a studio on the Avenue
Victor Hugo. First solo show in Prague in 1947. Then shows
at the Galerie Niepce (1951) and the Galerie Arnaud (1952, 1954,
1956), the Galerie Saint-Laurent, Brussels (1955 and 1956); the
Meltzer Gallery, New York (1956). Salons: May, since 1949,
October 1952-53; « Nouvelles Réalités » (1956). Numerous group
exhibits, in France and abroad. Fénéon scholarship 1955.*

I know hardly any painting like that of Huguette Arthur-Ber-
trand, from which the world, with all its inspirations, appears wholly
excluded and which has its source only in the artist himself.
Huguette expresses her ideas and her emotions, her sorrows and her
joys, without seeking any final formulae which, on the contrary,
change with her. Her characteristic element of expression is the
line, which plays with color and subdues it.

There was a moment when the need to establish a sure order
predominated ; then the lines were neatly arranged and assigned to
geometric planes that corresponded in a well thought-out balance.
But the day came when all this calculation could no longer be justified, when it became more imperative to give free rein to impulse, to
let the hand act without subjecting it to amy law or rule. The
strokes became more alert, they curved and broke, they would pile
up to one side and disperse on the other. Color would filter in
among them or oppose them in detached planes. Today the
dynamic forces prevail. The lines rush on one another, seek en-
counters without finding them, and as they palpitate become lost
in the void. Glimpses of bright tints appear amid the dark streaks,
illuminated by flashes of vivid colors that slip in among them. The
gates of the universe are opened wide, but the artist who has forced
them has discreetly hidden herself.

H. W.

TINSUR - *40″ × 32″ - 1956.*

CAMILLE

Born in Constantine (Algeria). Came to Paris very young, continued her studies and at the same time attended free drawing and painting courses at the Grande Chaumière.

Formed bonds of friendship with Rebeyrolle, Dmitrienko, Landzman, Rezvani, Thomson.

The group separates and each one goes in a different direction; Camille exposes her first works in the successive salons of "Artists under Thirty"...

Her painting at this time was figurative, but already transposed in a highly original way: still lifes, portraits, compositions of figures. There followed a slow but unmistakable evolution in the direction of non-figurative art.

She gave her first solo show at the Galerie Arnaud in 1952. Her canvases were gay, very colorful, with vibrant blues, greens and pinks; great attention was always given to paint quality.

They could be described as sensitive and poetic building games. "Camille plays at landscapes", is the critics' comment.

Camille has participated in the following group shows: Galerie de Babylone, 1952 ; Galerie Kléber, 1955 ; Galerie Octobon, Saint-Paul de Vence, 1955 ; Galerie La Roue: "Eloge du Petit Format", 1955 ; Galerie Arnaud, 1956 ; Galerie Bernheim Jeune, 1956 ; Galerie Intérieurs, Angers, 1956 ; Salon de Mai et Festival de l'Art d'Avant-Garde, Cité Radieuse, Marseille, 1956.

R. M.

ENAMELS - 36" × 24" - 1956.

OSCAR CHELIMSKY

Born January 5, 1923, in New York. Studied in New York at Cooper Union, the Delevante Studio, from 1939 to 1943, and at the Art Students' League in 1945. Has lived in Paris since 1948. Has exhibited, in group shows, in Europe and in America. In Paris, Galerie Jeanne Bucher since 1952. Has taken part in the May Salon, in the « October », « Nouvelles Réalités », « Comparaison » salons. Canvases at the Guggenheim Musuem and the Paris Museum of Modern Art. Private collections in New York, Detroit, Brussels, Paris, etc.

If Chelimsky uses a sign as a starting point, it is an *open* sign, a pure injunction of life on the canvas, a call to the second sign and the multitude of signs that, from one to the next, occupy the whole space. Thus is constituted a language of a perfect plastic intelligibility which itself lets itself be absorbed in the totality of the painting. Upon the spacious struggle of the sign with the sign are superposed and combined, distributed over the whole surface, innumerable conflicts, sources of energy, principles of harmony, which engender the movement, maintain the tensions and develop. Among these the contest of white with black asserts itself insistently. The moment those whites appear, which they usually do, those flows of lime that seem to emerge dreamily from the canvas and the intimacy of the night, the line of charcoal, alert and resolute, comes running from outside, responds and becomes enamoured. A strange lyrical couple, distinct and joined, like sleep and the dance. Color, playing the rôle of medium and mediator, multiplies its vibrations, its glidings, its subtle dissonances, under the hegemony of a dominant shade.

But if Chelimsky's great compositions penetrate us with an irresistible feeling of fullness and of freedom, they owe it perhaps to the presence of the void that is incorporated, as though in counterpoint, in the play of forms and colors and the invisible articulation of the signs.

J. D.

PAINTING - 64" × 45" - 1956.

CORNEILLE

Born in Liège in 1922, of Dutch parents.   Attended drawing courses at the Academy of Fine Arts.   Worked at painting on his own.   First one-man show in 1946.   Co-founder of the Dutch experimental group Reflex in 1947.   Founding member in Paris, in 1948, of the international « Cobra » group.   Contributed to all the exhibits of this movement.   Principal one-man shows : Europa Iskola, Budapest, 1947 ; Galerie Martinet, Amsterdam, 1951 and 1954 ; Galerie Horemans, Antwerp, 1951 ; Het Venster, Rotterdam, 1951 and 1955 ; Galerie Colette Allendy, 1953 and 1954 ; Venice Biennial 1954 ; Sao Paulo Biennial 1954 ; Galerie Craven, 1956 ; Palais des Beaux-Arts, Brussels, 1956 ; Amsterdam Musuem of Modern Art, 1956 ; Municipal Museum of Schiedam, 1956 ; S. Guggenheim Foundation Prize for Holland 1956.

On the occasion of the exhibition at the Martinet Gallery, in Amsterdam, in 1954, six young Flemish and Dutch poets each dedicated a poem to Corneille, collected in a booklet, "Sextet voor Corneille".   This is a translation of "Hugo Claus's Tribute to the painter Corneille":

> When the birds and the spirals,
> when the articulations had revolted,
> they left their meadows, their virgin rocks,
> for the warm house of hides,
> and Corneille, He-who-gyrates,
> inhabiting it, exclaimed:
>
> "Your heart (that spiderweb) is my heart.
> Salute the bird-catcher, o parrots !"
>
> Santeuil and flea market approved.
> Nerves and filaments unknotted their dryads.
>
> That all this in truth took place
> was discussed
> by the travelers of the sands, the seducers of the night.
> with the cries of men decapitated, with amazement,
> with gentle rains.
>
> HUGO CLAUS.

WALK IN THE AFTERNOON - *32" × 26" - 1956.*

JACQUES DOUCET

Born in 1924 in Boulogne-sur-Seine. Finished secondary school.
Lives in Paris, by his painting. Has never pursued any other occup-
ation. Principal exhibits in France: Galerie Colette Allendy and
Galerie Ariel. « Les Mains Eblouies » (Maeght); Divergences (Galerie
Arnaud); May Salon; Painting Biennial, Marseille. Holland:
Amsterdam Museum of Modern Art. Belgium: Museum of Liège,
Palace of Fine Arts, Brussels. Exhibits in Switzerland, Italy, Ger-
many, Austria, Hungary, United States (French section of the Car-
negie Prize).

Jacques Doucet belongs to the freest generation, to the most
demanding also, that whose coming to consciousness rose from the
ruins, immediately after the war. Jacques Doucet is a free man
because he was an adolescent hunted by Nazism. His first commitment was as a hostage at the Santé prison, his first freedom was
being associated with Max Jacob. His first and only adherence to
the French experimental tradition and his reasoned liberation, he
owes to Mrs. Colette Allendy, as he owes his tempering of his native
violence to Jean Pollak, who had the tact to leave him his utter
truculence. And so it is my privilege to have before my eyes paintings that bear witness to a conscious effort that breaks away from
the imperatives of time. By an act of will, this man is so free that
he appears a libertarian, this artist is so entire that he appears brutal.
Through mastery, he achieves in his life and in his work a state of
isolation, as it were, without shackle and without concession, which
leaves him alone, and consequently unique.

JACQUES GAMBIER DE LAFORTERIE.

PAINTING - CXX - *29" × 24" - 1956.*

ROGER EDGARD GILLET

Born July 10, 1924, in Paris. Has Flemish blood in his veins. 1939: Ecole Boulle. 1944: École des Arts Décoratifs. 1946-1948: teacher at the Ecole Jullian. First one-man show at the Galerie Evrard, Lille, in April 1953; in November of the same year, at the Galerie Craven. Since then: March, 1954, Galerie La Licorne, Brussels, and in October 1956, Galerie Ariel, Paris... Numerous group expositions, including: « Signifiants de l'Informel » and « Un Art Autre » by Michel Tapié (1953), « Phases », by Edouard Jaguer (1954 and 1955), October and May Salons, etc. Fénéon and Gatherwood fellowhips.

Here, then, art and painting rediscover one of their capital powers, if it is among the most distant and most lost. No human gesture, in the last analysis, is devoid of meaning, but art—by which we may here understand the encounter, harmonious perhaps but first passional, of desire and form—has the privilege of making the effective gesture, and better, of renewing this gesture within a cycle that is surely more and more ample, but thereby all the more perfectly centered, or in which what is called style and its "figures" become progressively effaced to the point of becoming indistinguishable from the gestures and the acts—the figures, in a word, of a ritual that is the very dialogue of man, and the plastic form of this dialogue, with the characters who inhabit it.

Gillet's painting, if one takes it as it is, is by birth and vocation inhabited by such characters.

And the style of his painting, its quality and I might even say its spiritual odor, are embodied in this approach, now obscure, now sparkling, to that most mysterious part of ourselves, as modern men, in which a strange being, obsessed by his own myth, has not yet despaired of finding the rites and the words that give the sun and push back the night.

Gillet's painting is the place of one of these rites.

CHARLES ESTIENNE (1953).

PAINTING - *40" × 29" - 1956.*

ROBERT LAPOUJADE

He was born in Montauban, January 3, 1921, and he has never got over his surprise at being here. 1947: first figurative exhibit at the Galerie Jeanne Castel. 1949: portraits of various literary figures (Eluard, Sartre, Claudel, etc.) First exhibit of abstract art, entitled « Prétextes et peinture formelle » accompanied by a manifesto that has the dimensions of an essay : « Le Mal à Voir » (the difficulty of seeing). A period marked by elementary investigations, beginning with « l'Informe ». 1951 : « Compositions » at the Galerie de Babylone; Lapoujade here manifested the desire to give his painting a « meaning »: 1952 : « L'enfer et la mine », at the Galerie Arnaud, an exhibit constituting a response to a certain « social realism ». Since then, new investigations and the publication of a theoretical book, « Les Mécanismes de Fascination » (Editions du Seuil).

"Painting is a reality that has all the earmarks of being natural, but at the price of circumventing the real and of creating the sense of it by imposing its own signs and its own laws. By virtue of this, every plastic sign, magic potentially and in fact, by its (human) nature, can signify any meaning whatever, on condition that it be seized, organized and finally made constitutive of a reality that is the very proof of this meaning and its new form. (To this we must add the role of color: a suggestive role, which also obeys laws of harmony and coherence.)

"All painting today takes its chances on this manifestation of interference between man and the world to make a new meaning appear, by contention and by the deepening of an already accepted comprehensive meaning: a permanent effort at coming to awareness, which perhaps is orientated toward a super-awareness—a kind of final reception of consciousness in its own completion, in the illusion of absolute knowledge, the temptation to be everything."

50

THE HORSES - 58" × 35" - 1956.

JOHN LEVEE

Born April 10, 1924, in Los Angeles, California. Exhibited in Europe for the first time in 1950. Took part in 1951 in the May Salon and in the Automn Salon. Exhibited at the Galerie Huit, Paris. 1954 : one-man exhibit at the Landau Gallery, Los Angeles, and at the Het Venster Gallery, Rotterdam ; the same year, May Salon. 1955 : Phases of Contemporary Art, Paris ; fifty years of Art in the U.S.A., Musée d'Art Moderne in Paris ; May Salon, and one-man exhibit at Gimpel Sons, in London. 1956 : Galerie de France, May Salon and « Nouvelles Réalités » salon. Work in numerous private collections in France and abroad, and in the Bâle Museum, Smith College Museum, Mass., New York Museum of Modern Art, Museums of Amsterdam, Carnegie Institute, Pittsburgh, Cincinnati.

If John Levee's first Parisian canvases (1950) are compared with the works he has done recently, one is struck first by the clearcut evolution that has led the painter from a reinvented figurative universe to an art without literal reference to any kind of representation of the external world.

But it is also possible to feel, as a background to the technical progress, to the evolution of forms, to the enrichment of human experience, how fundamentally exacting Levee's art has always remained.

This exactingness, opposed to any scholasticism, measures at every moment the creative spontaneity of the painter by the powers of the paint quality, of color and light.

A universe is thus created, with its own originality, its dramatic resonances. And with all the possibilities of transformations and of fidelity to himself that we may feel him to possess at the same time.

GUY MARESTER.

PAINTING - 24" × 18" - 1956.

MARYAN

Born January 1st in sub-Carpathian Poland. Without nationality. Settled for good in Paris in 1950. Two years at the Ecole des Beaux-Arts. First one-man exhibit at the Galerie Breteau in 1951. Then, at the Galerie Saint Placide (1952), Galerie 25 (1953), Galerie Le Miroir, Brussels (1954), Galerie Breteau (1955), Museum of Tourcoing (1956). Took part in 1951 and 1952 in the Salon des Surindépendants, then in the May Salon from 1953. Numerous group exhibits, including « 10 Young Painters of the Paris School » at the Galerie de France in 1956.

Maryan has derived his inspiration and his themes from the reality that was immediate and that had everyday familiarity for him. But this reality is excessively stylized ; it becomes expressive, dramatic in its expression. "A drama must occur in a painting", says Maryan himself. And a drama actually does occur in all his canvases.

By what means? That is the whole question. The element of drawing is very accentuated with Maryan, and his apprenticeship as a lithographer has not been lost. Wide, thick strips of black, sometimes opaque, at other times transparent, replace what was a line ; the contour has become body... Characters armed with mandibles and pincers remind one of sorcerers and insects. Nails, iron fittings, hooks provide them with a barbarous jewelry...

A new Chagall. That, if one will, is Maryan. A Chagall of our time. As hard, as violent, as impenetrable as Marc Chagall was and remains tender, open and seductive.

JEAN GRENIER.

54

PAINTING - *46" × 35" - 1956.*

LOUIS NALLARD

Nallard was born June 17, 1918, in Algiers of French parents. Of Burgundian peasant descent. Secondary and musical schooling in Algiers. Began to paint at the age of twelve, exhibited at sixteen. 1946: first abstract paintings. 1947: won « La Bataille » prize at Drouant-David's; settled in Paris. 1950 and 1951: Fénéon scholarship. Exhibited at the Salon des Moins de Trente Ans, « Réalités Nouvelles », etc. Numerous group exhibits. Canvases at the Galerie Jeanne Bucher.

It may be said of Nallard that after Mondrian he is Braque's most direct heir. Not by school descent, by the superficial borrowing of the cubist technique, but by the profound similarity of their pictorial approach, by the singular authenticity of their presence, by their common fidelity to Cézanne. Braque, a cubist, reconstructs the world on a quartered guitar, emptying the object to the point of denying it, to make it be more personal in another light, weight and fullness. Nallard, an abstractionist, builds beyond all appearance, a universe grasped at the source and at the wholly lived completion of the act of seeing. But for both the canvas is the willed, total expression of a man, slowly engendered by his very work. It thus possesses the continual density of an unfaltering tension, the rigor and the bearing of an organic development. A spiritual space with disconcerting structures, it is a coextensive inner vision of the very forms that make it manifest itself in the world, taking charge of existence even to metamorphosis. Cruelly present in its anxious becoming, its high discretion, its brotherly enigma even, the canvas lyrically incarnates the inevitable concern with being.

C. KRIEF.

PAINTING - 29" × 20" - 1954.

KUMI SUGAÏ

Sugai was born in 1921 in Kobe, Japan. Studies at the Ecole des Beaux-Arts (traditional art and European art). Came to Europe in 1954 and settled in France. Exhibited at the Galerie Craven and at the Galerie Remac, in Antibes. In Japan, which he left because he could not express himself freely there, his influence on young painters is now very great, and he is imitated by many. He has participated in group exhibits and in the principal salons of the new painting.

Sugaï is Japanese, which means that he is first of all a poet, and refined, infinitely attentive to detail, which he knows how to enlarge, to isolate. But in Sugaï the Malayan element undoubtedly dominates. And his refinement is not devoid of a strong dose of primitivism. His world is the world of flowers, of petals, of corollas, of pebbles, but also of demons, of masks, of magic dolls.

There would have been something lacking in the young Paris School if Sugaï had not come and joined it. At the same time, this Japanese needed Paris, in order to be able to realize himself as a Japanese painter, just like that Pole, that Swiss, that Italian, and all those who have found in Paris what they brought with them: themselves...

Sugaï has learned especially from Klee, from Miro: we are, however, familiar with the skill of the Japanese in assimilating western technique, and how they subsequently use it with originality. In fact, Sugaï has a position all his own, on the extreme frontier of the "*dépaysage*" (departure from the familiar) of the non-figurative painters, and the genii and the devils of his childhood do not allow his being labeled "abstract": They never weary, indeed, of reappearing, in the nacre-colored paint, right in the middle of the picture, sowing a little triangle of sharp red here, which is a dragon's tooth, or thrusting out a claw, or displaying a moustache...

Play, vision, magic, Sugaï's world is the world of wonder. The least form, in each of his paintings, is endowed with a strange life ; this is an animist art...

JEAN-CLARENCE LAMBERT.

YAMATO - *40″ × 29″ - 1956.*

ARBITER LIGHT BACKGROUND - *29" × 24" - 1956.*

WILFRID MOSER

Born in Zurich in 1914. Came to Paris in 1945. Worked at André Lhote's and at Fernand Léger's. Took up abstract painting in 1949. One-man show: Galleria la Cittadella, Ascona, 1954. May Salon, 1954. Groups: Galerie Jean Bucher, 1952-1955. Kunsthaus, Zurich, 1949. Stockholm, Lausanne, Zurich, 1951. New York, Berne, Bâle, Cologne, 1953. « Divergences », Galerie Armant, 1954-1956. Galerie Craven, « Six Paintres Actuels », 1955.

As Moser's painting does not propose any definable subject, it should necessarily be classified under abstract art. However, for those who do not let themselves be deceived, his canvases taken together form a great book of pictures, in which are reflected towns and landscapes, one does not know whether the painter has seen them or dreamed them, or if he has heard their melancholy history. Sometimes we perceive the night space through porous and crumbled walls, transparent despite numerous superimposed layers. Sometimes we catch an odd tang of virgin forest, we find ourselves in an anguishing jungle from which only those who can cut their way through emerge alive. But the darkness may brighten at any moment, with the light hiding in all the cracks ready to burst forth.

It is his anxiety that impels this artist to paint, and not the joy of creating. But the force that dictates his path is imperious, and if he is born to battle with the devil and God, who are probably identical, his painting derives from this a profound sincerity.

HERTA WESCHER.

56